The Gluten-Free Cookbook

"A Comprehensive Guide to Gluten-Free Cooking and Baking"

Peter Miller

Table Of Content

INTRODUCTION

The Gluten-Free Cookbook: A Comprehensive Guide to Gluten-Free Cooking and Baking" is a must-have for anyone looking to adopt a gluten-free diet or just looking to incorporate more gluten-free meals into their routine. This cookbook is a comprehensive guide that covers everything from the basics of gluten-free cooking and baking to more advanced techniques and ingredients.

The book begins with an introduction to gluten and why a gluten-free diet is necessary for some people. It then goes on to explain the different types of gluten-free flours and ingredients that can be used in cooking and baking, as well as tips and tricks for successfully substituting traditional wheat flour with gluten-free alternatives.

The bulk of the book is dedicated to the delicious and nutritious recipes, which cover a wide range of meal types, including breakfast, snacks, main dishes, and desserts. Each recipe includes a list of ingredients, easy-to-follow instructions, and beautiful photographs to inspire your cooking. Whether you're new to gluten-free cooking or an experienced cook, you'll find a variety of recipes to suit your taste and skill level.

In addition to the recipes, the book also includes a comprehensive resource section that provides information on where to find gluten-free ingredients, as well as tips for eating out and traveling on a gluten-free diet.

"The Gluten-Free Cookbook: A Comprehensive Guide to Gluten-Free Cooking and Baking" is an essential guide for anyone looking to live a healthy and delicious gluten-free lifestyle. With its clear and concise instructions, beautiful photographs, and tasty recipes, this cookbook will make it easy to create delicious and nutritious meals that everyone in your family will love.

CHAPTER ONE
Introduction to Gluten-Free Cooking and Baking

In this chapter, we will discuss the basics of gluten-free cooking and baking, including an overview of gluten, why a gluten-free diet is necessary for some people, and the different types of gluten-free flours and ingredients that can be used in cooking and baking.

First, we will discuss gluten and its role in our diet. Gluten is a protein found in wheat, barley, and rye. It is what gives bread and other baked goods their characteristic texture and chewiness. However, for some people, consuming gluten can cause a variety of health problems, including celiac disease, gluten intolerance, and wheat allergies. A gluten-free diet is necessary for these individuals to manage their symptoms and maintain their health.

Next, we will discuss the different types of gluten-free flours and ingredients that can be used in cooking and baking. Some popular gluten-free flours include almond flour, coconut flour, and rice flour. These flours can be used in a variety of recipes, from cakes and cookies to breads and pizzas. Additionally, there are a variety of gluten-free ingredients that can be used as substitutes for traditional wheat-based ingredients, such as xanthan gum, which can be used to thicken sauces and bind dough.

Finally, we will provide tips and tricks for successfully substituting traditional wheat flour with gluten-free alternatives. This includes information on how to properly measure and combine gluten-free flours, as well as how to adjust the texture and consistency of gluten-free baked goods. With the information and guidance provided in this chapter, you will be able to create delicious and nutritious gluten-free meals that everyone in your family will love.

CHAPTER TWO
Breakfast Recipes

In this chapter, we will provide a variety of delicious and nutritious gluten-free breakfast recipes, including pancakes, waffles, breakfast burritos, frittatas, oatmeal, and smoothies. These recipes are easy to make and are sure to please everyone in your family.

1. Gluten-Free Pancakes

- 1 cup gluten-free flour blend
- 1 tablespoon sugar
- 2 teaspoons baking powder
- 1/4 teaspoon salt
- 1 egg
- 1 cup milk (dairy or non-dairy)
- 2 tablespoons melted butter or oil
- 1 teaspoon vanilla extract

In a large mixing bowl, combine the gluten-free flour blend, sugar, baking powder, and salt. In a separate bowl, beat the egg, then add the milk, melted butter or oil, and vanilla extract. Add the wet ingredients to the dry ingredients and mix until just combined. Heat a non-stick skillet or griddle over medium-high heat and pour 1/4 cup of batter for each pancake. Cook until bubbles form on the surface and the edges start to dry, then flip and cook for an additional 1-2 minutes. Serve with your favorite toppings.

2. Gluten-Free Waffles

- 1 1/2 cups gluten-free flour blend
- 2 tablespoons sugar
- 2 teaspoons baking powder
- 1/4 teaspoon salt
- 1 egg
- 1 1/4 cups milk (dairy or non-dairy)
- 1/4 cup melted butter or oil
- 1 teaspoon vanilla extract

In a large mixing bowl, combine the gluten-free flour blend, sugar, baking powder, and salt. In a separate bowl, beat the egg, then add the milk, melted butter or oil, and vanilla extract. Add the wet ingredients to the dry ingredients and mix until just combined. Preheat a waffle iron and pour 1/2 cup of batter for each waffle. Cook until golden brown and crispy. Serve with your favorite toppings.

3. Gluten-Free Breakfast Burrito

- 1/2 cup cooked and crumbled gluten-free breakfast sausage.

- 1/2 cup diced bell peppers.

- 1/2 cup diced onions.

- 1/2 cup diced potatoes.

- 4 eggs, beaten.

- 1/4 teaspoon salt

- 1/4 teaspoon pepper

- 4 gluten-free tortillas

- 1/2 cup shredded cheese.

- Salsa and avocado for topping

In a skillet over medium heat, sauté the breakfast sausage, bell peppers, onions, and potatoes until cooked through. Add the beaten eggs and season with salt and pepper. Cook until the eggs are set, then remove from heat. Warm the gluten-free tortillas in the microwave or on a skillet. Divide the egg mixture among the tortillas, then top with shredded cheese. Roll up the tortillas to form burritos. Serve with salsa and avocado on top.

4. Gluten-Free Frittata

- 1/2 cup cooked and crumbled gluten-free breakfast sausage.

- 1/2 cup diced bell peppers.

- 1/2 cup diced onions.

- 1/2 cup diced potatoes.

- 8 eggs, beaten.

- 1/4 teaspoon salt

- 1/4 teaspoon pepper

- 1/2 cup shredded cheese.

Preheat the oven to 375 degrees F. In a skillet over medium heat, sauté the breakfast sausage, bell peppers, onions, and potatoes until cooked through. Add the beaten eggs and season with salt and pepper. Cook until the eggs are set, then remove from heat. Sprinkle shredded cheese over the top of the frittata. Place the skillet in the preheated oven and bake for 10-15 minutes, or until the cheese is melted and the frittata is fully cooked. Remove from the oven and let it cool for a few minutes before slicing and serving.

5. Gluten-Free Oatmeal

- 1 cup gluten-free rolled oats.

- 1 cup milk (dairy or non-dairy)

- 1/2 cup water

- 1/4 teaspoon salt

- 1/4 cup chopped nuts (optional)

- 1/4 cup dried fruit (optional)

- 1 tablespoon honey or maple syrup (optional)

In a medium saucepan, bring the milk, water, and salt to a boil. Add the gluten-free rolled oats and reduce the heat to medium-low. Cook, stirring occasionally, for 5-7 minutes, or until the oats are soft and creamy. Remove from heat and stir in chopped nuts, dried fruit, and honey or maple syrup, if desired. Serve warm and enjoy.

6. Gluten-Free Smoothie

- 1 cup frozen berries (strawberries, blueberries, raspberries)

- 1 banana

- 1/2 cup yogurt (dairy or non-dairy)

- 1/2 cup milk (dairy or non-dairy)

- 1 tablespoon honey or maple syrup (optional)

- 1/4 cup gluten-free rolled oats (optional)

In a blender, combine the frozen berries, banana, yogurt, milk, honey or maple syrup, and gluten-free rolled oats, if desired. Blend on high speed until smooth and creamy. Pour into a glass and enjoy.

These are some examples of gluten-free breakfast recipes that you can try, you can make variations and experiment with different ingredients to make it more delicious and suit your taste.

CHAPTER THREE
Snack and Appetizer Recipes

In this chapter, we will provide a variety of delicious and nutritious gluten-free snack and appetizer recipes, including crackers, chips, dips, spreads, and appetizer dishes. These recipes are easy to make and are perfect for entertaining or for satisfying a quick hunger between meals.

1. Gluten-Free Crackers

- 1 cup gluten-free flour blend
- 1/4 teaspoon salt
- 1/4 teaspoon pepper
- 1/4 cup grated cheese (optional)
- 1/4 cup chopped herbs (optional)
- 2 tablespoons olive oil
- 1/4 cup water

Preheat the oven to 350 degrees F. In a mixing bowl, combine the gluten-free flour blend, salt, pepper, grated cheese, and chopped herbs (if using). Add the olive oil and water, and mix until a dough forms. Roll out the dough on a lightly floured surface to about 1/8 inch thickness. Use a knife or a pizza cutter to cut the dough into cracker-sized pieces. Place the crackers on a baking sheet lined with parchment paper. Bake for 12-15 minutes or until golden brown. Let them cool before serving.

2. Gluten-Free Chips

- 1 large potato, peeled and sliced thinly
- 2 tablespoons olive oil
- 1/4 teaspoon salt
- 1/4 teaspoon pepper

Preheat the oven to 400 degrees F. In a mixing bowl, toss the potato slices with olive oil, salt, and pepper. Spread the potato slices on a baking sheet lined with parchment paper. Bake for 15-20 minutes or until crispy and golden brown. Let them cool before serving.

3. Gluten-Free Dip

- 1 cup cooked and mashed sweet potato
- 1/2 cup plain yogurt (dairy or non-dairy)
- 1/4 cup chopped fresh cilantro
- 1/4 teaspoon cumin powder
- 1/4 teaspoon salt
- 1/4 teaspoon pepper

In a mixing bowl, combine the cooked and mashed sweet potato, yogurt, cilantro, cumin powder, salt, and pepper. Mix well. Taste and adjust the seasoning as needed. Serve the dip with gluten-free crackers or chips.

4. Gluten-Free Spread

- 1 can of chickpeas, drained and rinsed
- 1/4 cup tahini
- 2 cloves of garlic, minced
- 2 tablespoons lemon juice
- 1/4 teaspoon salt
- 1/4 teaspoon pepper

- 3 tablespoons olive oil

- Water as needed

In a food processor, combine the chickpeas, tahini, garlic, lemon juice, salt, and pepper. Process until smooth. Slowly add the olive oil while the food processor is running. Add water as needed to achieve the desired consistency. Taste and adjust the seasoning as needed. Serve the spread with gluten-free crackers or chips.

5. Gluten-Free Meatballs

- 1 pound ground beef or turkey

- 1/4 cup grated parmesan cheese

- 1 egg

- 1/4 cup gluten-free bread crumbs

- 1/4 cup chopped parsley

- 1/4 teaspoon salt

- 1/4 teaspoon pepper

In a mixing bowl, combine the ground beef or turkey, parmesan cheese, egg, gluten-free bread crumbs, parsley, salt, and pepper. Mix well. Form the mixture into small meatballs. Heat a skillet over medium heat and cook the meatballs until browned and cooked through. Serve the meatballs with your favorite gluten-free dipping sauce

6. Gluten-Free Fried Rice

- 1 cup gluten-free jasmine rice
- 2 cups water
- 1/4 teaspoon salt
- 2 tablespoons vegetable oil
- 1/2 cup diced carrots
- 1/2 cup diced celery
- 1/2 cup diced onions
- 2 cloves of garlic, minced
- 2 eggs, beaten
- 1/4 cup gluten-free soy sauce
- 1/4 cup chopped green onions

Rinse the gluten-free jasmine rice in a fine mesh strainer under cold running water. In a medium saucepan, bring the water to a boil.

Add the rice and salt. Stir, cover, and reduce heat to low. Cook for 18 minutes or until the water is absorbed and the rice is tender. Remove from heat and fluff the rice with a fork. Let it cool.

In a large skillet or wok, heat the vegetable oil over high heat. Add the diced carrots, celery, and onions. Stir-fry for 2-3 minutes or until the vegetables are tender. Add the garlic and stir-fry for 30 seconds. Push the vegetables to one side of the skillet and pour the beaten eggs into the empty side. Scramble the eggs until cooked. Add the cooked rice, gluten-free soy sauce and green onions. Stir-fry for 2-3 minutes or until the rice is heated through. Serve the fried rice with your favorite gluten-free protein or as a side dish.

These are some examples of gluten-free snack and appetizer recipes that you can try, you can make variations and experiment with different ingredients to make it more delicious and suit your taste.

CHAPTER FOUR
Main Dish Recipes

In this chapter, we will provide a variety of delicious and nutritious gluten-free main dish recipes, including pasta dishes, pizza, chicken, beef, fish and vegetarian and vegan options. These recipes are easy to make and are perfect for dinner or special occasions.

1. Gluten-Free Pasta

- 8 ounces gluten-free spaghetti
- 1 cup gluten-free marinara sauce
- 1/2 cup grated parmesan cheese
- 1/4 cup chopped fresh basil
- Salt and pepper, to taste

Cook the gluten-free spaghetti according to package instructions. Drain and set aside. In a saucepan, heat the gluten-free marinara sauce over medium heat. Add the cooked spaghetti and toss to coat. Remove from heat and sprinkle with parmesan cheese, basil and salt and pepper. Serve hot.

2. Gluten-Free Pizza

- 1 gluten-free pizza crust
- 1/2 cup gluten-free marinara sauce
- 1/2 cup shredded mozzarella cheese
- 1/4 cup grated parmesan cheese
- 1/4 cup sliced mushrooms
- 1/4 cup diced bell peppers
- 1/4 cup diced onions
- 2 cloves of garlic, minced
- 1/4 teaspoon dried oregano
- Salt and pepper, to taste

Preheat the oven to 425 degrees F. Place the gluten-free pizza crust on a baking sheet lined with parchment paper. Spread the gluten-free marinara sauce over the crust, leaving a 1/2-inch border around the edges. Sprinkle the shredded mozzarella cheese, parmesan cheese, mushrooms, bell peppers, onions, garlic, oregano, salt and pepper over the sauce. Bake for 15-20 minutes or until the crust is golden brown and the cheese is melted. Remove from the oven and let it cool for a few minutes before slicing and serving.

3. Gluten-Free Chicken Parmesan

- 4 boneless, skinless chicken breasts
- 1/2 cup gluten-free bread crumbs
- 1/4 cup grated parmesan cheese
- 1/4 teaspoon dried oregano
- 1/4 teaspoon dried basil
- Salt and pepper, to taste
- 1/4 cup gluten-free marinara sauce
- 1/2 cup shredded mozzarella cheese

Preheat the oven to 375 degrees F. In a shallow dish, combine the gluten-free bread crumbs, parmesan cheese, oregano, basil, salt, and pepper. Dip the chicken breasts in the mixture, pressing the mixture onto the chicken to coat. Place the chicken on a baking sheet lined with parchment paper.

Bake for 25-30 minutes or until cooked through. Remove from the oven and top each chicken breast with gluten-free marinara sauce and shredded mozzarella cheese. Return to the oven and bake for an additional 5-10 minutes, or until the cheese is melted and bubbly.

4. Gluten-Free Beef Stir Fry

- 1 pound flank steak, thinly sliced
- 2 tablespoons vegetable oil
- 1/2 cup sliced onions
- 1/2 cup sliced bell peppers
- 1/2 cup sliced mushrooms
- 2 cloves of garlic, minced
- 1/4 cup gluten-free soy sauce
- 1/4 cup beef broth
- 1 tablespoon cornstarch
- 1/4 teaspoon ground ginger
- Salt and pepper, to taste

In a small bowl, whisk together the gluten-free soy sauce, beef broth, cornstarch, ginger, salt, and pepper. Set aside. In a large skillet or wok, heat the vegetable oil over high heat. Add the sliced flank steak and stir-fry for 2-3 minutes or until browned. Remove the beef from the skillet and set aside. In the same skillet, add the sliced onions, bell peppers, mushrooms, and garlic. Stir-fry for 2-3 minutes or until tender. Add the beef back to the skillet, along with the soy sauce mixture. Cook, stirring constantly, until the sauce thickens, about 2-3 minutes. Serve over rice or noodles.

- Gluten-Free Fish Tacos

- 1 pound cod or tilapia fillets

- 1/4 cup gluten-free flour

- 1/4 teaspoon cumin powder

- 1/4 teaspoon chili powder

- Salt and pepper, to taste

- 2 tablespoons vegetable oil

- 8 gluten-free corn tortillas
- 1/2 cup shredded cabbage
- 1/4 cup chopped cilantro
- 1/4 cup diced tomatoes
- 1/4 cup diced avocados
- 1/4 cup gluten-free sour cream
- Lime wedges, for serving

In a shallow dish, combine the gluten-free flour, cumin powder, chili powder, salt, and pepper. Dredge the fish fillets in the mixture, shaking off any excess. In a large skillet, heat the vegetable oil over medium-high heat. Add the fish fillets and cook for 3-4 minutes per side, or until golden brown and cooked through. Remove the fish from the skillet and set aside.

Warm the gluten-free corn tortillas in the microwave or on a skillet. To assemble the tacos, place a piece of fish on each tortilla, then top with shredded cabbage, cilantro, tomatoes, avocados, and a dollop of gluten-free sour cream. Serve with lime wedges on the side.

6. Gluten-Free Vegetarian and Vegan Recipes

- 1 cup cooked quinoa
- 1 can black beans, drained and rinsed
- 1/2 cup corn kernels
- 1/4 cup diced red onion
- 1/4 cup chopped cilantro
- 2 tablespoons lime juice
- 1 tablespoon olive oil
- Salt and pepper, to taste

In a large bowl, combine cooked quinoa, black beans, corn, red onion, cilantro, lime juice, olive oil, salt and pepper. Mix well. Taste and adjust the seasoning as needed. Serve as a main dish or as a side dish.

These are some examples of gluten-free main dish recipes that you can try, you can make variations and experiment with different ingredients to make it more delicious and suit your taste.

CHAPTER FIVE
Dessert Recipes

In this chapter, we will provide a variety of delicious and nutritious gluten-free dessert recipes, including cakes, cookies, pies, tarts, ice cream, and sorbet. These recipes are easy to make and are perfect for satisfying a sweet tooth or for special occasions.

1. Gluten-Free Chocolate Cake

- 1 1/2 cups gluten-free flour blend
- 1 cup granulated sugar
- 3/4 cup cocoa powder
- 2 teaspoons baking powder
- 1/2 teaspoon baking soda
- 1/2 teaspoon salt
- 1 cup milk (dairy or non-dairy)
- 2 eggs
- 2 teaspoons vanilla extract

- 1/2 cup vegetable oil

Preheat the oven to 350 degrees F. Grease and flour a 9-inch round cake pan. In a large mixing bowl, combine the gluten-free flour blend, sugar, cocoa powder, baking powder, baking soda, and salt. In a separate bowl, whisk together the milk, eggs, vanilla extract, and vegetable oil. Add the wet ingredients to the dry ingredients and mix until just combined. Pour the batter into the prepared cake pan and bake for 25-30 minutes, or until a toothpick inserted in the center comes out clean. Let the cake cool in the pan for 10 minutes before transferring it to a wire rack to cool completely.

2. Gluten-Free Chocolate Chip Cookies

- 1 cup gluten-free flour blend
- 1/2 teaspoon baking powder
- 1/4 teaspoon baking soda
- 1/4 teaspoon salt
- 1/2 cup (1 stick) unsalted butter, at room temperature

- 1/2 cup granulated sugar

- 1/2 cup brown sugar

- 1 egg

- 1 teaspoon vanilla extract

- 1 cup gluten-free chocolate chips

Preheat the oven to 350 degrees F. Line a baking sheet with parchment paper. In a medium mixing bowl, whisk together the gluten-free flour blend, baking powder, baking soda, and salt. In a large mixing bowl, beat the butter, granulated sugar, and brown sugar together until light and fluffy. Beat in the egg and vanilla extract. Gradually add the dry ingredients to the wet ingredients and mix until just combined. Stir in the chocolate chips. Drop the dough by rounded tablespoons onto the prepared baking sheet. Bake for 12-15 minutes or until golden brown. Let the cookies cool on the baking sheet for 5 minutes before transferring them to a wire rack to cool completely.

3. Gluten-Free Apple Pie

- 1 gluten-free pie crust

- 6 cups peeled, cored and thinly sliced apples

- 3/4 cup granulated sugar

- 2 tablespoons gluten-free flour

- 1/2 teaspoon ground cinnamon

- 1/4 teaspoon ground nutmeg

- 1/4 teaspoon salt

- 2 tablespoons butter

Preheat the oven to 375 degrees F. Roll out the gluten-free pie crust and press it into a 9-inch pie dish. In a large mixing bowl, combine the apples, sugar, gluten-free flour, cinnamon, nutmeg, and salt. Pour the mixture into the pie crust and dot with butter. Place the pie on a baking sheet and bake for 45-50 minutes, or until the crust is golden brown and the filling is bubbly. Let the pie cool before serving.

4. Gluten-Free Sorbet

- 2 cups fresh berries (strawberries, raspberries, blue berries, or a combination)

- 1/2 cup granulated sugar

- 1/2 cup water

- 1/4 cup fresh lemon juice

In a medium saucepan, combine the berries, sugar, and water. Cook over medium heat, stirring occasionally, until the sugar is dissolved, and the berries are soft. Remove from heat and let cool. Once cooled, transfer the mixture to a blender and blend until smooth. Strain the mixture through a fine-mesh sieve to remove any seeds. Stir in the lemon juice. Cover and refrigerate the mixture until cold, about 2 hours or overnight. Churn the mixture in an ice cream maker according to the manufacturer's instructions. Transfer the sorbet to a container and freeze until firm, about 2 hours.

5. Gluten-Free Ice Cream

- 2 cups heavy cream

- 1 cup whole milk
- 3/4 cup granulated sugar
- 1 teaspoon vanilla extract
- 1/4 teaspoon salt
- 5 large egg yolks

In a medium saucepan, combine the cream, milk, sugar, vanilla extract, and salt. Cook over medium heat, stirring occasionally, until the sugar is dissolved. In a medium mixing bowl, whisk the egg yolks. Slowly pour the hot cream mixture into the yolks, whisking constantly. Return the mixture to the saucepan and cook over low heat, stirring constantly, until the mixture thickens and coats the back of a spoon. Strain the mixture through a fine-mesh sieve into a large mixing bowl. Cover and refrigerate the mixture until cold, about 2 hours or overnight. Churn the mixture in an ice cream maker according to the manufacturer's instructions. Transfer the ice cream to a container and freeze until firm, about 2 hours.

These are some examples of gluten-free dessert recipes that you can try. You can make variations and experiment with different ingredients to make it more delicious and suit your taste. Whether you're looking for a sweet treat to enjoy after dinner or a dessert to bring to a party, these gluten-free recipes are sure to please. From cakes and cookies to pies and ice cream, there's something for everyone in this chapter. So, go ahead and indulge in these delicious and gluten-free desserts.

CHAPTER SIX
Resources

In this chapter, we will provide information and resources for those on a gluten-free diet. We will cover where to find gluten-free ingredients, tips for eating out and traveling on a gluten-free diet, and suggestions for further reading and resources.

1. Finding Gluten-Free Ingredients

- Many supermarkets now carry a wide variety of gluten-free products in the natural foods or health food section.

- Online retailers such as Amazon and Thrive Market also offer a wide selection of gluten-free products.

- Specialty health food stores and co-ops often carry gluten-free products, as well as other alternative flours and ingredients.

- Many health food stores carry gluten-free flours, breads, crackers, pasta, and other products.

2. Eating Out and Traveling on a Gluten-Free Diet

- When eating out, always inform the server of your dietary restrictions and ask about gluten-free options.

- Look for restaurants that specialize in gluten-free or have dedicated gluten-free menus.

- When traveling, research gluten-free options at hotels and restaurants before arriving.

- Pack gluten-free snacks and meals for the plane or car ride.

3. Further Reading and Resources

- The Gluten-Free Alliance - A non-profit organization dedicated to raising awareness about gluten-free issues and providing resources for those on a gluten-free diet.

- Gluten-Free Living - A magazine that provides news, information, and resources for those on a gluten-free diet.

- Gluten-Free Girl - A website that provides recipes, tips, and resources for those on a gluten-free diet.

- Gluten-Free Dietitian - A website that provides nutrition advice and resources for those on a gluten-free diet.

These are just a few examples of the many resources available to those on a gluten-free diet. With a little research and planning, it's possible to enjoy delicious and nutritious meals while adhering to a gluten-free diet.

CHAPTER SEVEN
Conclusion

In this book, we have provided an overview of gluten and the importance of a gluten-free diet for some individuals. We have also provided a variety of delicious and nutritious gluten-free recipes for breakfast, main dishes, snacks, desserts, and more.

The key takeaways from this book are:

- Gluten is a protein found in wheat, barley, and rye, and a gluten-free diet is necessary for individuals with celiac disease or gluten intolerance.

- Gluten-free cooking and baking can be delicious and satisfying with the use of alternative flours and ingredients.

- With a little research and planning, it's possible to enjoy delicious and nutritious meals while adhering to a gluten-free diet.

We encourage you to continue experimenting with gluten-free cooking and baking. Try different flours and ingredients, and don't be afraid to make substitutions in your favorite recipes. With a little creativity, you'll be amazed at the delicious and satisfying meals you can create while following a gluten-free diet.

In conclusion, following a gluten-free diet can provide many benefits for those with celiac disease or gluten intolerance, including improved digestion, increased energy, and overall improved health. We hope this book has been a helpful guide in your gluten-free journey, and we wish you all the best in your continued exploration of gluten-free cooking and baking.